Deborah

The highest form of worship is obedience.

PHYLLIS J. STEVENS

Andrew Kilcup
Illustrator

ILLUMIFY MEDIA GLOBAL
Littleton, Colorado

Deborah

Published by
Illumify Media Global
www.IllumifyMedia.com
"Let's bring your book to life!"

Paperback ISBN: 978-1-959099-27-7

Typeset by Art Innovations (http://artinnovations.in/)
Cover design by Andrew Kilcup

Printed in the United States of America

To my daughters,

Samara, and Alexandra.

My granddaughters,

Sierra, Angelina, Chantel, Malaika, Kenadee and Mya.

My great granddaughters,

Jaelyn, Angel, and Braylen.

"For you are a people holy to the Lᴏʀᴅ your God. The Lᴏʀᴅ your God has chosen you to be a people for His *treasured possession*, out of all the people who are on the face of the earth."

Deuteronomy 7:6 (ESV, emphasis added).

Contents

Foreword

The story of Deborah is about a courageous woman who help others recognize the power and strength to conquer mountains in their lives.

Deborah caused others to rise. She believed everyone had a purpose. She challenged those around her to fight for themselves, family, and future generations.

My auntie (Phyllis Stevens) is a modern-day Deborah. In our family, she has stood up, stretched her hand, and helped us to Rise Up! Her daughters, granddaughters, nieces, and future generations will rise and intentionally walk in God's purpose.

Thank you, Auntie — You have blessed my life!

Dr. Nicoa Garrett, PhD

Preface

In the book of Joshua, in the Bible, God tells Joshua to finish the job that Moses started, to lead His people into Canaan, the Promised Land. In other words, take the land. This is the land that God had promised to give Abraham, because Abraham had faith enough to leave everything to follow God.

The war between the people of God and Canaan was not a war just over gaining land or power. This was God judging Canaan's sins and their idolatrous religion. By taking the land of Canaan God would do two things; He would judge the Canaanites for their sin against Him and fulfill His promise to Abraham.

Before Moses died, God would speak to Moses. Moses would tell God's word to His people, "When the Lord your God delivers them [the Canaanites] over to you, you shall conquer them and totally destroy them. You shall make no covenant with them nor show mercy to them" (Deuteronomy 7:2, NKJV).

God saw that the people of Canaan had stubborn hearts and that they were not willing to repent and turn to Him. The Canaanites built idols for their gods. To please their gods, they did horrible things that the Lord hated. They were even sacrificing their children to the fire to please their gods.

DEBORAH

*"You shall not worship the L*ord *your God in that way, for every abomination to the L*ord *which He hates they have done to their gods; for they have even burn their sons and their daughters in the fire to their gods"*
(Deuteronomy 12:31).

After Moses' death, God used Joshua to lead His people. Following many years of fighting God gave Israel the land of Canaan. Joshua left nothing undone of all that the Lord commanded Moses.

"So, Joshua took the whole land, according to all that the Lord had spoken to Moses. And Joshua gave it for an inheritance to Israel according to their tribal allotments. And the land had rest from war."
(Joshua 11:23)

Before Joshua died, he warned the people what will happen if Israel stop clinging to God:

- God would no longer fight for them.
- The Canaanites would be like snares and traps, whips to lash them, thorns that fly back into their faces, stabbing their eyes.
- Miseries and troubles would increase until they are perished from the good ground that the Lord their God has given them.

Joshua died without appointing a new leader.

It wasn't long before Israel compromised, they didn't completely obey, they did not drive the Canaanites out, instead they lived among them and made them slaves.

Israel's disobedience meant that it could no longer be a recipient of the promised blessings.

By the time you get to the book of Judges, Israel is living in the midst of the Canaanites, they are intermarrying (Judges 3:6) with the Canaanites and serving their gods (Judges 3:7).

"But whenever the judge died, they [Israel] turned back and were more corrupt than their fathers, going after other gods, serving them, and bowing down to them"
(Judges 2:19).

They were:
- Worshiping in pagan gardens and consulting with the dead.
- Disregarding God's dietary laws.
- They had become religiously arrogant.

"So the anger of the LORD was kindled [hot] against Israel and He gave them over to plunderers (robbers) who plundered them; and He sold them into the hands of their surrounding enemies, so that they could no longer withstand their enemies"
(Judges 2:14).

Deborah

The book of Judges is named after a collection of individuals who God used to lead His people after the death of Joshua. The role of a Judge is a term for leadership.

In this time of national decline, despite their promise to keep the covenant (Joshua 24:16-18), the people turned from the Lord and began to worship other gods. "Everyone did what was right in his own eyes."

The judges of Israel were primarily military and civil leaders. Deborah was a military commander as well as a judge and prophetess for God's people.

A prophetess or prophet is a person that God spoke to during these days. Deborah would take the message that God has given her, and she would tell it to the people.

DEBORAH

For twenty years, the Canaanites oppression was severe against the Israelites because of their superior military force of 900 iron chariots under the command of Sisera from Harasheth Haggoyim. These chariots had two large wheels. They were open behind and carried a driver, a warrior, and a shield bearer. Sisera was the captain of Jabin, the Canaanite king's army.

The Canaanites had stripped Israel from most of its weaponry (Judges 5:8). Even if they wanted to fight, they had little to fight with. The Canaanites had iron chariots, shields, spears, and other things they made into weapons (Judges 5:8).

1

God Tells Deborah to Fight

The people of Israel lived in villages outside the walled city of the Canaanites. They lived in fear every day, because of Sisera and his army. They were too afraid to come out of their homes for any reason other than food and supplies. The village roads were empty. Village life had stopped. No casual shopping. No children playing outside. No taking walks. Everything stopped. If they needed food or supplies, they would never use the main roads, they would stay out of sight and sneak along the bypaths. They would hurry and get what they needed then hurry back home.

~~~~~~~~~~

Deborah, a prophetess who fully followed the Lord, was the wife of Lappidoth. She was the judge of Israel at the time. She held court under a palm tree in the mountains of Ephraim, approximately nine miles north of Jerusalem. All Israel came up to her to have their disagreements heard.

DEBORAH

When the cruelty became so great, the children of Israel would cry out to the Lord for help. The Lord would always raise up a deliverer for His people. This time God called Deborah.

The Spirit of the Lord came upon Deborah to deliver His people. Deborah immediately sent and called for Barak a warrior, from the town of Kedesh in Naphtali which is 100 miles north of Ephraim. It takes Barak three days to reach Deborah.

Deborah looks at Barak and says, "Has not God of Israel commanded you to go gather 10,000 of your men from Naphtali and Zebulun, troops from the northern tribes. You are to take them to the top of Mount Tabor. And I, the Lord, will draw out Sisera the general of Jabin's army to fight against you by the river Kishon. He will bring his chariots and his troops. Then I will give him and his army into your hand."

God choose Mount Tabor because He knew it would be hard for Sisera's chariots and army to climb up hill. Mount Tabor rises to 1,300 feet and was located at the juncture of Naphtali and Zebulun where Barak would get his troops from.

The message from God to Barak was that He, God would be in sovereign control of the battle.

Barak listens to all that God has said through Deborah. He knew that Deborah was a prophetess. He wanted to be assured of God's divine presence while in battle. He says to Deborah, "If you will go with me, then I will go. But if you do not go, I will not go!"

Deborah did not hesitate to respond to Barak, "Surely, I will go with you. But because of the way you are going about this, the victory will not lead to your glory. It will be given to a woman."

Even though Barak did not hasten to immediately obey God's calling, he is named with the heroes of faith in Hebrews 11:32.

2

The Battle

Deborah arose early and went with Barak to Kedesh. When they arrived, Barak sent messengers to the tribes of Zebulun and Naphtli. The message was to gather all their warriors and anything they could use as weapons and meet him on top of Mount Tabor. It didn't take long before 10,000 men were heading to meet Barak and Deborah.

Heber, a Kenite now living in Canaan, hears noises and looks out his tent and sees thousands of men walking with weapons toward Mount Tabor. He calls to one of the men, "What is happening?"

"Barak and Prophetess Deborah has called us to fight."

Heber is a descendant of Moses' father-in-law. When Moses was leading God's people to the Promised Land, he invited his father-in-law to come with them (Num. 10:29). Moses promised his father-in-law Jethro/Reuel/Habab (he was called by all three names in Exodus and Numbers) that God would bless him if he came.

THE BATTLE

Over time Moses' father-in-law's descendants left the living God for the gods of the Canaanites. They did not care that God had said, "You shall not worship the Lord your God in that way, for every abominable thing that the Lord hates they have done for their gods, for they even burn their sons and daughters in the fire of their gods" (Deuteronomy 12:31).

By this time Heber had been serving the Canaanite's king for years. He waited until all the men had passed his tent and out of sight before running to warn Jabin. When Jabin heard of the Israelite's plans, he called for Sisera. As Sisera listened to his king, his eyes turned like shards of glass, hard and cutting.

THE BATTLE

Sisera was so angry when he heard that Israel was planning an attack, that he told his commanders to ready all 900 of his chariots of iron and his warriors and foot soldiers. His plan was to destroy them all. It took several hours before they were ready to march to the river Kishon.

Deborah and Barak saw the dust from so many horses and chariots long before they saw Sisera and his army. As Sisera and his army were approaching the Kishon River, Deborah yelled to Barak, "Up! For this is the day in which the LORD has given Sisera into your hand. Does not the LORD go out before you?" (Judges 4:14).

DEBORAH

Barak turned to his warriors, and when he lifted his spear in the air, his 10,000 men started to shout and lift their weapons and tools they were using as weapons in the air. Barak turned back around and charged down Mount Tabor against the much stronger forces of Sisera.

The minute Barak and his army started down Mount Tabor, an unseasonal and violent rainstorm started. The rain was so fierce that it caused the waters of the Kishon River, where Sisera's army was approaching to overflow.

When Sisera saw the Israelite's army coming towards them, he was so determined to destroy Israel that he ignored the overflowing river. He started hitting his horses even more to make them move faster. When he reached the Kishon River the chariots started to slow down. Iron chariots were very heavy. They were not made to go up mountains. By this time Mount Tabor's steep and uneven roads were wet and slippery. As much as Sisera beat his horses the chariot could not move any faster. The wheels were mired in the deep mud. Horses began to slip in the mud, pitching men off into the river. Some of the foot soldiers did eventually reach the mountain and tried to climb. Many fell face down in the puddles at the base of the hill. Even if they got up the mountain a short distance, they soon lost their footing and fell back down. God was fighting for His people.

This gave enough time for Barak and his men to reach the chariots and foot soldiers.

THE BATTLE

Sisera's soldiers were trying to fight against the wind, rain and the Kishon River, as well as God's people.

Barak saw that God was fighting for Israel. He knew that God had given them the victory. Barak and his army killed many with the edge of the sword. When Sisera's army saw that the war was lost they turn and ran. Barak continued to chase them until Sisera's entire army was destroyed.

3

The Flight and Death of Sisera

When Sisera saw his army being killed all around him, he knew that he was defeated. He jumped from his chariot and began to flee from the battle on foot. He ran toward the tents of Heber the Kenite, who had a friendly relationship with Jabin the king.

Jael looks out her tent and sees Sisera running for his life. She calls to him, "Turn aside, my lord; turn aside to me, do not be afraid." Sisera thinking that Jael, Heber's wife has the same friendly relationship with Jabin the king as her husband and that no one would look for him in a female's tent. With rain dripping from his face, he stops at her tent. He is exhausted, frustrated, and scared. Jael tells Sisera to come in. She looks around and sees a straw filled canvas. "Lie down and I will hide you under this canvas." Before settling down, Sisera asked, "Please give me a little water to drink for I am thirsty?" Jael opens a wineskin of milk and gives it to Sisera. He drinks greedily. When his thirst was satisfied, he said to Jael, "Stand at the opening of the tent, and if any man comes and ask you, "Is anyone here?" You tell them, "No."

THE FLIGHT AND DEATH OF SISERA

Jael was a Bedouin woman. Their job was pitching the tents once the people arrived at their new settlement.

After Sisera falls asleep, Jael went to where she kept her hammer and pegs. With a hammer and peg in her hand she walked quietly over to where Sisera was sleeping. She listens to his breathing. When she was sure that he was in a deep sleep, she bent down next to his head, places the tent peg near Sisera's temple and with one swing, drives the peg into his head. The force was so strong that it drove the peg though his temple into the ground.

Jael, stands up, turns her back on Sisera's body, and walks out the tent. The wind from the rain was whipping the tent flap about when she sees Barak and some of his army pursuing Sisera. She calls to Barak, "Come and I will show you the man whom you are seeking." Barak following her into her tent, sees Sisera's dead body with a tent peg in his temple.

Barak remembers what Deborah said, "I will surely go with you. Nevertheless, the road on which you are going will not lead to your glory, for the Lord will sell Sisera into the hand of a woman" (Judges 4:9).

Barak turns and open the flap of the tent. He notices that the heavy rain is now a drizzle. He calls out to three of his men, "You there, come and get the body of Sisera and put it with the other bodies." To the other men with him he says, "The rest of you go help with the wounded. Take them back to camp.

23

DEBORAH

THE FLIGHT AND DEATH OF SISERA

The army of Barak grew stronger and stronger against Jabin king of Canaan, until he had destroyed Jabin king of Canaan and the Canaanites forces were no longer a threat to Israel.

God subdued Jabin in the presence of the children of Israel.

4

The Victory Song
to Remember God's Goodness

Sisera was dead, the battle had ended, and the rain had stopped, Deborah and Barak, still wet with rain walked back to the battlefield. This gave them a chance to see the mighty works of the Lord.

They saw hundreds of chariots turned on their sides in the mud. Dead bodies of the Canaanite army everywhere. Some killed by the Israel army. Many killed when the chariots they were driving turned over and fell on top of them and the foot soldiers that were walking next to the chariots.

Once back at camp Deborah changes into dry clothes, then sits down on wet dirt under a low growing tree and meditates on the goodness of God. She was so overwhelmed with the goodness of God that she starts to sing. Her first thoughts were of the men who left their families and willingly came out to fight.

THE VICTORY SONG TO REMEMBER GOD'S GOODNESS

I praise the Lord for the leaders and volunteers who willingly by
faith, came out to fight against great odds.
Hear me, O kings, give ear and listen, O Princes, to the Lord I will
sing; I will make melody to the Lord, the God of Israel,

Psalm 66:8 says, "Bless our God, O peoples; let the sound of His praise be heard."

As she sits there, she starts to think back to Moses and his preparation to enter the Promised Land and how God displayed his power and majesty on Mount Sinai to the people. The people heard crashing thunder and a very loud trumpet blast. They saw lightning, fire, rain, and billowing smoke. The mountains trembled as in a violent earthquake. The black smoke brought darkness to the sky.

"Lord, when You went out from Seir when you marched from the
region of Edom, the earth trembled and the heavens dropped,
yes, the clouds dropped water. The mountain quaked before the
Lord, even Sinai before the Lord, the God of Israel"
(Judges 5:4-5).

DEBORAH

THE VICTORY SONG TO REMEMBER GOD'S GOODNESS

She sings about the distress and poverty that gripped Israel from the time of Shamgar, son of Anath, until now. She knows the cause of Israel's suffering is rooted in Israel's idolatry, "new gods were chosen" (Judges 5:8). She asks a question, *"Was shield or spear to be seen among forty thousand in Israel?"* The answer is no because the Israel's troops were disarmed during the time of oppression. A few weapons were secretly hidden away.

"In the days of Shamgar, son of Anath, in the days of Jael, the highways were abandoned, and travelers kept to the byways. Until I, Deborah, arose as a mother to Israel" (Shamgar was one of Israel's judges. He killed 600 Philistines with a wooden eight feet long tool, that had an iron spike at one end. The tool was used to spur on his oxen as they pulled his plow or his cart. It was called an Ox goad.)

Deborah again praises God because of the faithful leaders and volunteers among the people who responded in time of crises. Even though they had few real weapons. *"My heart goes out to the commanders of Israel."*

She wanted the rich nobles (*those who ride on white donkeys, who sit on rich carpets*) and the merchants, commoners and poor (*those who walk along the road*) to tell everyone of the goodness of God. Go tell the musicians who sets at the watering places, so they can put God's goodness to music. Then others will sing, the righteous triumphs of the Lord (Judges 5:8-11).

Deborah began to think about all the tribes that came to fight. She began to sing passionately how the Lord called her and Barak to fight.

DEBORAH

"Awake, awake, Deborah! Awake, awake, break out in song! Arise
Barak lead away your captives, O son of Abinoam. Then down
marched the remnant of the noble. The people of the Lord
marched down for me against the mighty"
(Judges 5:12-13).

Deborah acknowledges the people of Zebulun and Barak home tribe of Naphtali for sending 10,000 men to fight. More men than any other tribe. Both tribes knew the stakes were high and the risk was great. They were not afraid to die on the battlefield with Barak on behalf of the Lord against Sisera and his chariots.

The kings of the Canaanites came looking for victory and spoils of silver, but instead they met defeat, because from heaven the stars fought. God used the forces of nature against them.

"The kings came, they fought; then fought the kings of Canaan
at Taanach, by the waters of Megiddo; they got no spoils of silver.
From heaven and stars fought from their courses
they fought against Sisera"
(Judges 5:19-20).

5

Not All Marched with Deborah and Barak

Deborah blesses Ephraim, Benjamin, and Machir for responding quickly to the call to arms. Ephraim "root," lived in the central hill county previously occupied by the Amalekites. It would take days of walking to reach Deborah and Barak.

"From Ephraim their root they marched down into the valley, following you, Benjamin, with your kinsman. From Machir marched down, the commanders, and from Zebulun those who bear the lieutenant's staff. The princes of Issachar came with Deborah and Issachar faithful to Barak; into the valley they rushed at his heels"
(Judges 5:14-15).

Deborah paused, then thought of Reuben, Gilead, Dan and Asher, who ignored God and didn't come to help. She asked Reuben why he and his tribe stayed in the fields with their sheep, listening to the shepherds play their pipes.

She called out Gilead for staying in the land they were allotted and not crossing Jordan to help (the Reubenites, the Gadites, and the half-tribe of Manasseh, who lived on the other side of the Jordan River. Joshua 1:12-15).

The tribe of Dan lived on the coast and sold merchandise. They stayed with their ships. And Asher who also lived at the coast, stayed on their lot of land. These questions were to their shame.

"Why did you sit still among the sheepfolds, to hear the whistling for the flocks? Among the clans of Reuben there were great searching of heart. Gilead stayed beyond the Jordan, and Dan, why did he stay with the ships? Asher sat still at the coast of the sea, staying by his landings"
(Judges 5:16-17).

It is not Deborah but the Angel of the Lord who bitterly cursed Meroz inhabitants for failing to give aid. "Because they did not come to the help of the Lord, to help the LORD against the mighty" (Judges 5:23). Meroz people failed to come and help the Lord when He needed them. There is no greater failure than this.

6

Jael:
The Woman Who Killed Sisera

As a prophetess and representative of Yahweh, Deborah put to song the death of Sisera.

"Most blessed of women be Jael,
the wife of Heber the Kenite,
of tent-dwelling women most blessed.
He asked for water, and she gave him milk;
she brought him curds in a noble's bowl.
She sent her hand to the tent peg
and her right hand to the workmen's mallet;
she struck Sisera;
she crushed his head;
she shattered and pierced his temple.
Between her feet
he sank, he fell, he lay still;

DEBORAH

between her feet
he sank, he fell;
where he sank,
there he fell—dead"
—Judges 5:24-27

Despite Jael's husband Heber's peace agreement with King Jabin, Jael acted for the Lord and for God's people.

~~~~~~~~~~~~~~

After singing about Jael, Deborah starts to imagine that Sisera's mother is looking out her window wondering out loud, "Why is my son's chariot so long in coming? What has delayed him? I don't hear the hoofbeats of his horses."

She then looks to other for an answer, but they can give her none. She asks, "Have they not found and taken all the spoils by now? Is it so much loot to sort through that is taking the time? She was used to her son and his men ransacking the Israelites camps and nearby villages after a battle. "They should have already divided up the women, expensive cloth, and valuables."

Sisera's family and people were accustomed to him terrorizing the people of Israel.

"Out of the window she peered, the mother of Sisera wailed through the lattice: 'Why is his chariot so long in coming? Why tarry the hoofbeats of his chariots?' Her wisest princesses answer, indeed, she answers herself, have they not found and divided the spoil? —A womb or two for every man; spoil of dyed materials for Sisera, spoil of dyed materials embroidered, two pieces of dyed work embroidered for the neck as spoil?' "
(Judges 5:28-31).

7

Cursing and Blessings

Deborah being filled with the presence of God says, "So may all your enemies perish, O Lord! But your friends be like the sun as he rises in his might" (Judges 5:31).
Under Deborah's leadership, the land had rest for forty years.

~~~~~~~~~~~~

Would you like to know the one true God? The only way to know Him is through His Son Jesus Christ.

"For God so loved the world (you) that He gave His only begotten
Son (Jesus), that whoever believes in Him
should not perish but have everlasting life.
For God did not send his Son into the world to condemn the world.
But that the world through Him might be saved."
John 3:16-17

Would you like to know how the Israelites got into the land of
Canaan, or about Samson, another one of God's judges? Then read
Joshua, A Warrior For God
and
Samson, God's Rebellious Champion

by Phyllis J. Stevens
www.authorphyllisjstevens.com